The GIRLS' GUIDE to DRAWING

Revised and Updated Edition

W9-BDH-233

by Clara Cella and Kathryn Clay

Illustrated by June Brigman, Sydney Hanson, Cynthia Martin, Julia Nielsen, Anne Timmons, and Lisa K. Weber

CAPSTONE PRESS
a capstone imprint

TABLE OF CONTENTS

HELLO, ARTIST!

WELCOME TO YOUR PRIVATE ART CLASS! Whether you're a notebook doodler or an artist with a capital "A," you'll find tons of projects to love in here. What would you like to draw first? A puppy playing fetch? A prince on horseback? How about a blooming rose or a portrait in the style of artist Pablo Picasso? A unicorn, a pixie, or a 1970s retro outfit?

After you've picked your project, follow the simple step-by-step instructions. Some projects and steps are trickier than others. Take your time, and practice, practice, practice. Be sure to check the little idea bubbles for ways to take your drawings in new directions and make them your own!

HAVE FUN!

Tools and Supplies

Before you begin your drawing projects,
gather the following tools and supplies:

PAPER
Any type of blank, unlined paper will do.

PENCILS
Pencils are the easiest to use.
Make sure you have plenty of them.

SHARPENER
You'll need clean lines, so keep
a pencil sharpener close by.

ERASER
Pencil erasers wear out very quickly.
Get a rubber or kneaded eraser.

DARK PEN/MARKER
When your drawing is finished, you can
trace over it with a black ink pen or a thin
felt-tip marker. The dark lines will really
make your work pop.

COLORED PENCILS
If you decide to color your drawings,
colored pencils usually work best.

BABY ANIMALS

QUESTION: COULD THIS SECTION BE ANY CUTER? ANSWER: NO! Ten of the sweetest baby animals have crawled, hopped, and skipped onto the following pages. And they've done so for one reason—to have their portraits drawn by you!

SO much cute in here: You'll find a chick, a bunny, a piglet, a panda cub. . . . There's even a baby turtle with a fish friend. Turn the page to learn how to draw these bright-eyed, cuddly creatures step-by-step. Soon you'll be turning blank sheets of paper into one big stack of "Aww"!

CHICK

Look at that round, fluffy body and that tiny beak! Cute, right? Well, not everyone thinks so. Some people have a very real fear of chickens. This rare condition is called *alektorophobia* (ah-LEK-tohr-oh-FOH-be-ah). But don't worry. The chick you draw will *not* hurt you. Promise!

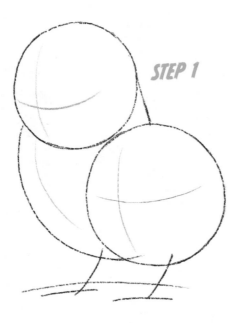

STEP 1

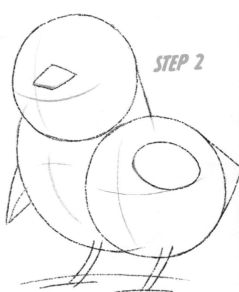

STEP 2

STEP 3

STEP 4

Try drawing a brood (group) of four or more little chicks.

STEP 5

"Good things come in small packages." Green sea turtle hatchlings are proof that this saying is true. They're about as long as your pinky finger when they start their lives in the ocean. But then they grow! Most adults measure 3 feet (91 centimeters) long and weigh more than 300 pounds (136 kilograms).

STEP 1

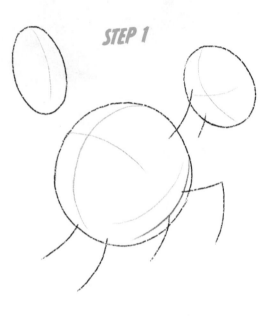

STEP 2

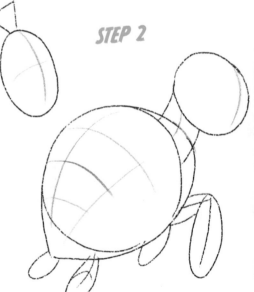

STEP 3

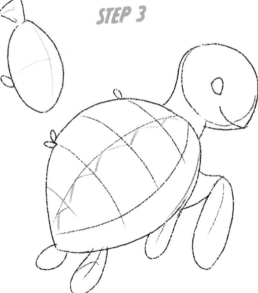

STEP 4

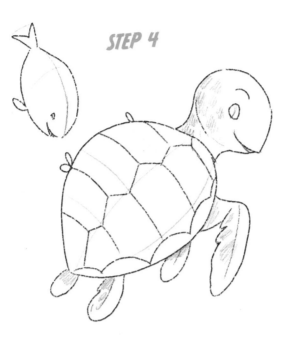

Once you've drawn this hatchling, draw another one with a wild pattern on its shell. Try squiggles, flowers, or stars.

STEP 5

BUNNY

For their first few weeks of life, bunnies drink milk from their mother. After that, they eat solid foods. While rabbits *do* eat carrots, they also eat grasses, clover, seeds, roots, buds, tree bark, and garden veggies. Rabbits are herbivores—animals that eat only plants.

STEP 1

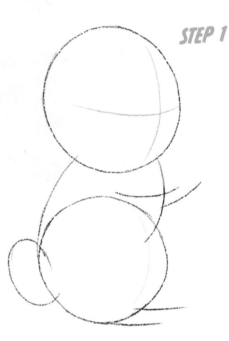

STEP 2

STEP 3

Draw a garden around your bunny, filled with leafy vegetables.

STEP 4

STEP 5

PANDA CUB

Why are giant pandas black and white? No one knows for sure. Some people think the colors help the animals hide. The black ears, eyes, nose, legs, and shoulders blend in with forest shadows. Other people think the markings are a way for pandas to know who's a panda and who's not!

STEP 1

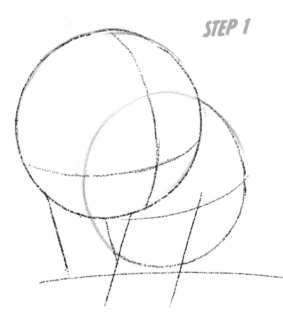

STEP 2

STEP 3

STEP 4

Pandas usually sit upright when they eat, like a person. See pages 164–165 to draw a panda chewing on a thick stem of bamboo.

STEP 5

RHINO CALF

See the horn on this calf? It gave rhinos their name! "Rhinoceros" comes from two ancient words meaning "nose horn." The horn is made of keratin—a material also found in fingernails, hair, claws, and hooves. Javan and Indian rhinos have one horn. Three other rhino species have two.

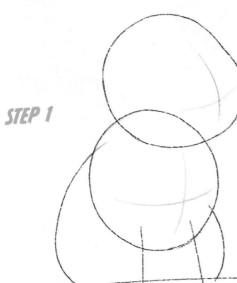

STEP 1

STEP 2

STEP 3

STEP 4

After drawing
your rhino calf,
draw another one
splashing in
a watering hole.

STEP 5

DONKEY FOAL

Like many animals, male and female donkeys have different names. Males are jacks. Females are jennies or jennets. In the wild, donkey herds usually have just one jack and a number of jennies. Donkeys like living in groups, but they may change herds from time to time.

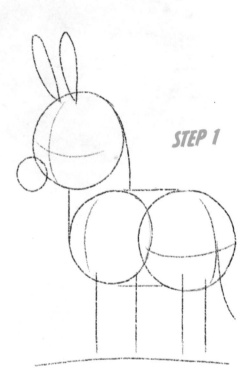

STEP 1

STEP 2

STEP 3

STEP 4

STEP 5

Donkeys are often used as pack animals. Try drawing a cart full of flowers for your donkey to pull.

PUPPY

More than 75 million pet dogs live in the United States. And they all started life the same way—as puppies! Newborn puppies can't see or hear for the first 10 days or so. They have no teeth. They spend nearly all day sleeping. But before long, they're ready to play!

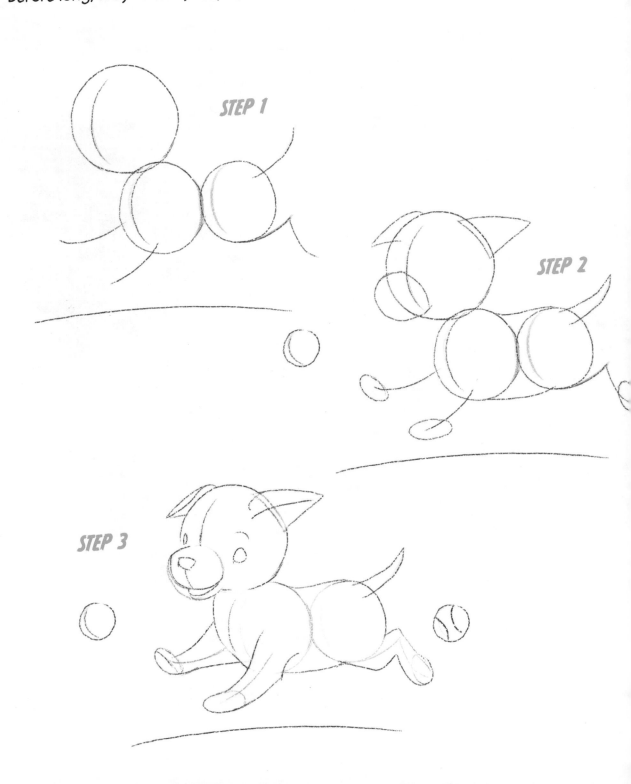

STEP 1

STEP 2

STEP 3

STEP 4

Draw yourself taking this puppy for a walk. Don't forget a leash!

STEP 5

ELEPHANT CALF

Big-time cute! Baby African elephants weigh an average of 250 pounds (113 kg) at birth. That's about the same weight as a refrigerator! Calves are not only able to stand within minutes of being born, but they can also walk after an hour or two.

STEP 1

STEP 2

STEP 3

STEP 4

Try drawing your elephant calf's mother. Make her tall enough so her baby can stand beneath her.

STEP 5

PIGLET

Shocking news: Pigs are some of the cleanest animals in the world! *But wait, you say. Don't they roll around in mud?* They do, but they roll in mud to cool off, not because they love getting dirty. Pigs can't sweat well. Wallowing in cool water or mud keeps them from overheating.

STEP 1

STEP 2

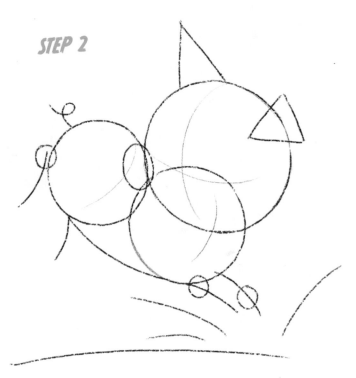

STEP 3

STEP 4

STEP 5

CONTINUED...

STEP 6

STEP 7

Keep your piglet cool! Draw it playing in a big, sloppy pool of mud.

STEP 8

CHEETAH CUB

Most of the world's wild cheetahs live on open grasslands in Africa. Their yellow coloring helps them blend in with the grasses. Patterns of black spots look like shadows. This camouflage allows adult cats to sneak up on prey. It also keeps cubs safe from predators such as lions and hyenas.

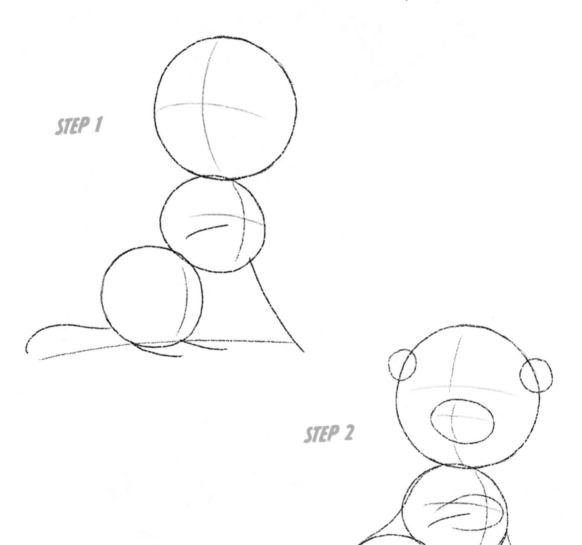

STEP 1

STEP 2

STEP 3

STEP 4

STEP 5

CONTINUED...

STEP 6

STEP 7

Try drawing your cheetah cub's mother. Keep her body lean and her legs long.

STEP 8

FLOWERS

WHAT'S ONE OF THE MOST POPULAR SUBJECTS TO PAINT? FLOWERS! Flowers come in all shapes, sizes, and colors, giving artists endless inspiration. Now it's your turn to create a floral masterpiece. Love bold blossoms that can't be missed? Draw a poppy. How about delicate designs? Sketch the tiny flowers on a lily of the valley. If traditional is more your style, give a rose a try.

You won't find every kind of flower in this section. But you will find nine projects that'll help you draw one beautiful garden!

TULIP

Tulips are prized for their unique styles. Some people even spend thousands of dollars on hard-to-find tulip varieties. For a basic tulip, draw a thick stem and a single flower with six petals. Then add long, waxy leaves.

STEP 1

STEP 2

STEP 3

STEP 4

Try creating your own tulip variety. Do the petals have pointed tips or ruffled edges?

STEP 5

ROSE

Roses are red. But they can also be white, pink, yellow, orange, or purple. With so many colors to choose from, it's easy to see why roses are a favorite. This rose includes a tight bud, a full-blown blossom, and, of course, a few thorns.

STEP 1

STEP 2

STEP 3

STEP 4

After drawing one rose, try drawing a big bouquet of multicolored roses in a tall vase.

STEP 5

POPPY

Wild poppies grow in giant fields that can be seen from miles away. Most people think of poppies as being a bright red color. But their paper-thin petals can also be white, pink, or purple.

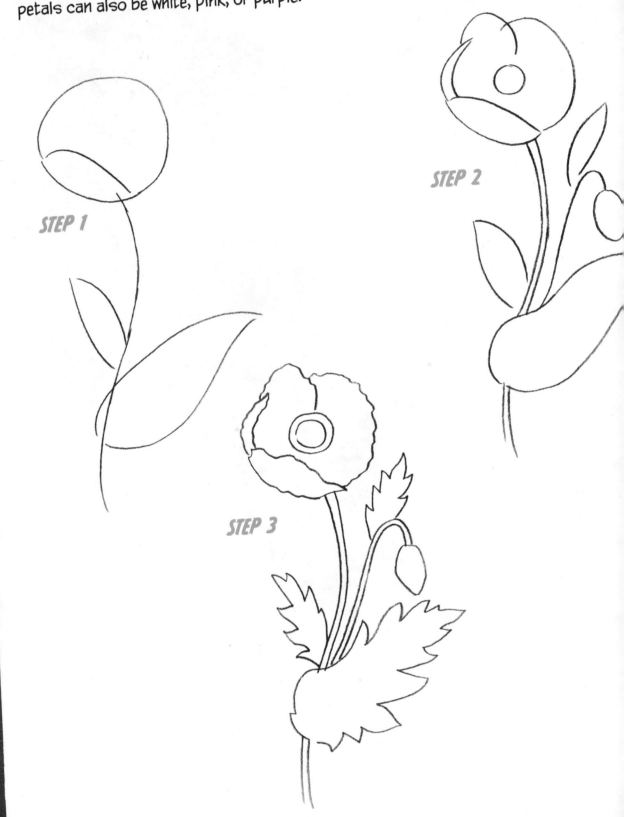

STEP 1

STEP 2

STEP 3

STEP 4

Once you've mastered one poppy, try drawing a large field filled with them.

STEP 5

DAISY

Daisies are hardy wildflowers that can grow just about anywhere. That's why they're sometimes considered weeds. To draw these daisies, start with a round center. Then add lots of skinny petals.

STEP 1

STEP 2

STEP 3

STEP 4

Try drawing a few
wild daisies growing
between the cracks
in a sidewalk.

STEP 5

CARNATION

Roses may be the most popular flower, but carnations are a close second. Carnations are long-stemmed flowers with ruffled petals. Their dainty petals make these flowers perfect for corsages.

STEP 1

STEP 2

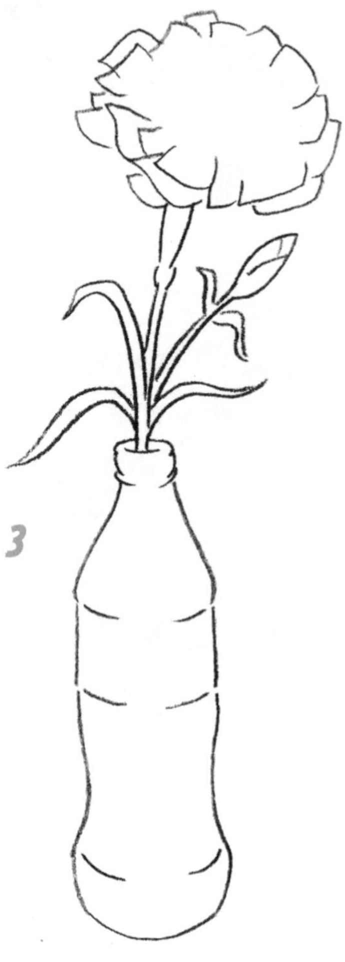

STEP 3

Try drawing a fancy corsage. Start with a carnation. Then add a few leaves, mini roses, and a ribbon.

STEP 4

STEP 5

Lily of the valley has small, bell-shaped flowers surrounded by pointy green leaves. This flower blooms in early spring. Its sweet smell attracts all kinds of birds and butterflies.

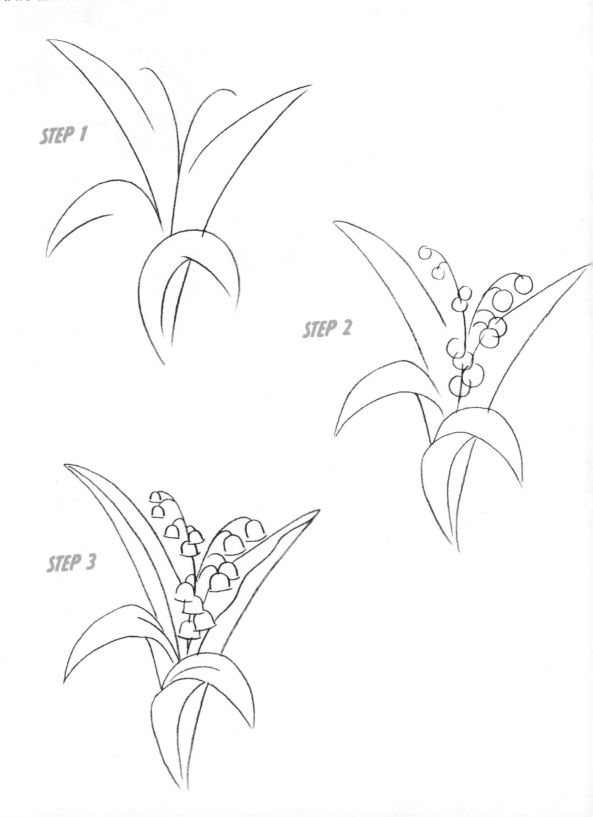

STEP 1

STEP 2

STEP 3

STEP 4

Draw a beautiful butterfly resting on a lily leaf.

STEP 5

SNAPDRAGON

Snapdragons are unusual flowers with an even stranger name. Each stem has a cluster of small flowers that resemble a dragon's mouth. Squeezing the sides of the snout-shaped flower creates a snapping sound.

STEP 1

STEP 2

STEP 3

STEP 4

Draw a window box filled with red, yellow, and pink snapdragons.

STEP 5

HYDRANGEA

Bees are always buzzing around giant hydrangea (hi-DRAIN-juh) blossoms. Hydrangeas are flowering shrubs filled with clusters of tiny flowers. Each small flower has four petals. Together these flowers can form blossoms up to 8 inches (20 cm) wide.

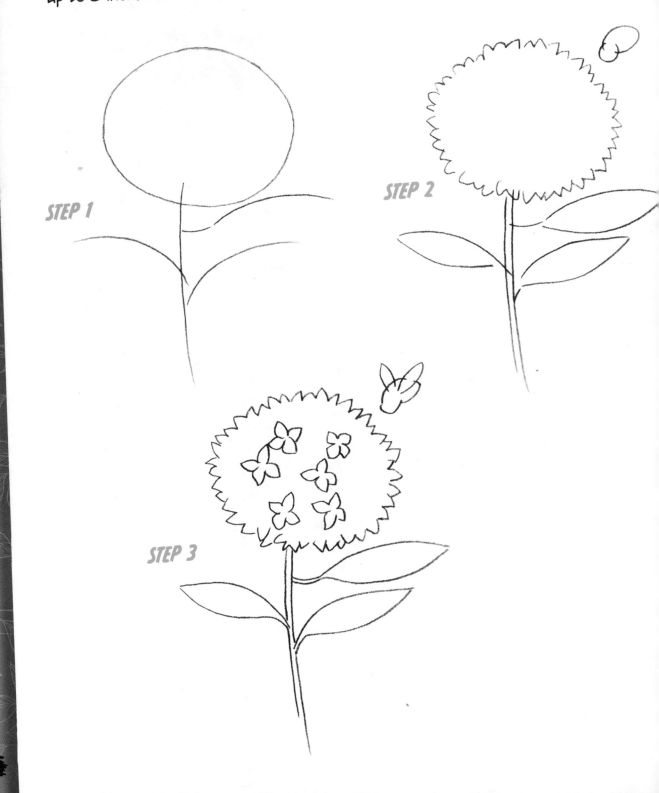

STEP 1

STEP 2

STEP 3

STEP 4

After drawing one hydrangea blossom, try drawing an entire shrub full of them.

STEP 5

FLOWER GARDEN

Now that you've practiced several flowers, try drawing them together as one colorful garden. Start with a big hydrangea shrub. Add a few tulips, daisies, carnations, poppies, and snapdragons. Then draw a fence to keep your garden safe from pests.

Maybe you love pansies or hollyhocks. Try drawing a garden filled with all of your favorite flowers.

STEP 1

STEP 2

STEP 3

CONTINUED...

STEP 4

STEP 5

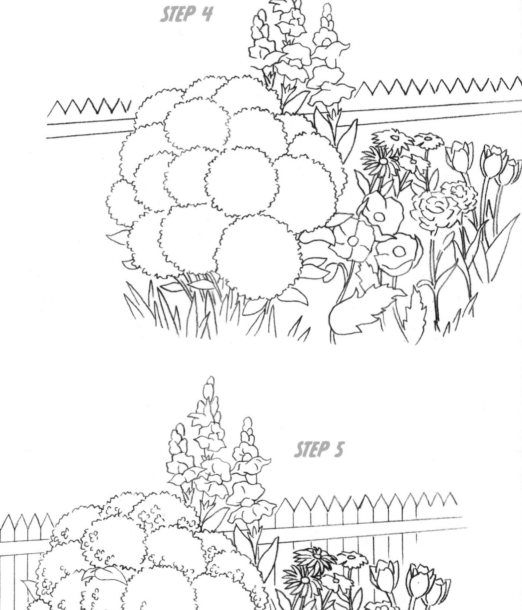

FAIRY TALES

ONCE UPON A TIME, THERE WAS AN AMAZING SET OF FAIRY-TALE DRAWING PROJECTS: THIS ONE!

You never know whom (or what) you'll meet in a fairy tale. A kind princess? A fearless prince? Maybe a beastly troll living under a bridge? In this section, you're about to meet all of these folks, plus six more. They've come from faraway, make-believe lands to have their portraits drawn by you. (A castle's ready for its close-up too.)

Turn the page to draw **HAPPILY EVER AFTER. . . .**

CASTLE

No fairy tale would be complete without a castle. With their stone walls and tall towers, castles are usually home to kings and queens. But all sorts of fairy-tale characters, including witches, can live in them too. If a castle is enchanted, a spell (good or bad) has been cast upon it.

STEP 1

STEP 2

STEP 3

STEP 4

Does your castle sit atop a snowy mountain or a grassy hill? Does it lie beneath the sea? Draw the surrounding area.

STEP 5

PRINCESS

Fairy-tale princesses come in all shapes, sizes, and colors. They're not always human, either! Hans Christian Andersen's little mermaid, for example, is part fish, part human. She's the daughter of the Sea King. And Princess Fiona, from the modern-day fairy tale "Shrek," is a creature called an ogress.

STEP 1

STEP 2

STEP 3

STEP 4

Once you've drawn your princess, add a pattern to her dress. Try flowers, stars, or swirls.

STEP 5

EVIL QUEEN

What's one thing all fairy-tale evil queens want? Power! They also want to be the most beautiful woman in the land. They lie, use magic, and sometimes harm others to get what they want. Two of the most famous evil queens appear in the stories "Snow White" and "Sleeping Beauty."

STEP 1

STEP 2

STEP 3

STEP 4

STEP 5

Anyone who drinks
this evil queen's
potion will turn into
a toad. Draw
a bunch of toads
at her feet.

FAIRY GODMOTHER

Fairy godmothers are imaginary beings who use magical powers to keep people safe and happy. With a flick of her wand, the fairy godmother in "Cinderella" turns rags into a beautiful gown. She turns a pumpkin into a carriage, mice into horses, and a rat into a coachman.

STEP 1

STEP 2

STEP 3

STEP 4

After you've drawn your fairy godmother, try drawing her again. This time, add bigger, fancier wings.

STEP 5

MERMAID

Don't challenge a mermaid to a swimming contest. Or a sing-off. You will lose both! Part fish, part human, fairy-tale mermaids have powerful tails that help them glide through the ocean. Their lovely singing voices have enchanted sailors around the world for thousands of years.

STEP 1

STEP 2

STEP 3

Draw a few underwater friends for your mermaid. Try some fish or a sea turtle. Or maybe an octopus.

STEP 4

STEP 5

OGRE

In traditional fairy tales, ogres (OH-gurz) are big and ugly. And they stink. Oh, and they eat people. They aren't the kind-hearted creatures you know from today's stories, like Shrek. Some of them have magical powers too. The ogre in "Puss in Boots" can change himself into any animal—from an elephant to a mouse.

STEP 1

STEP 2

STEP 3

STEP 4

STEP 5

After drawing your ogre, try drawing his wife. A female ogre is called an ogress.

TRICKSTER

Tricksters pop up in fairy tales all around the world. They play clever tricks to fool others out of their riches. Tricksters take many forms. Common animal tricksters include foxes, wolves, monkeys, rabbits, and spiders. One of the best-known tricksters? An odd little man named Rumpelstiltskin.

STEP 1

STEP 2

STEP 3

Once you've drawn your fox trickster, try drawing a sneaky partner for him—maybe a monkey or a rabbit.

STEP 4

STEP 5

WITCH

The witch smiles a sickly smile. Her bird looks like it knows a secret. Beware! Don't make the same mistake Hansel and Gretel made when the witch in their story offered treats. *Just say no.* Or you may wind up on the dinner menu!

STEP 1

STEP 2

STEP 3

STEP 4

Fairy-tale witches love magical spells and potions. Try drawing a large pot of bubbling potion for your witch.

STEP 5

PRINCE

When a classic fairy tale needs a hero, a handsome prince rides in. How does he save the day? He slays a giant or a fire-breathing dragon. He rescues a girl from a tower. He kisses a princess and breaks a witch's spell. Simple hero stuff.

STEP 1

STEP 2

STEP 3

STEP 4

CONTINUED...

STEP 5

STEP 6

Not all heroes look alike. Draw the horse again. But this time, draw the hero *you* want to see riding it.

STEP 7

TROLL

STEP 1

Think twice before crossing this ugly troll's bridge. He's mean and ready to gobble up anything in sight! Trolls first appeared in fairy tales from Norway and Sweden. In some of those stories, trolls came out only at night. If sunlight hit them, they turned into stone.

STEP 2

STEP 3

STEP 4

CONTINUED...

Try drawing the goats from the fairy tale "The Three Billy Goats Gruff" on top of the bridge.

STEP 5

STEP 6

STEP 7

HORSES

GRAB A PENCIL AND SADDLE UP! This section has a whole herd of horses for you to draw. Start out with a head study, then walk, trot, canter, and gallop your way through eight more projects. Love the heavy, muscular Clydesdales? The leaping Lipizzans? How about the breezy Arabians or the sure and steady Appaloosas? They're all in here, just waiting for you to BRING THEM TO LIFE!

(And when you get to the final project in this section? Draw your own face on the rider for some heart-pounding jumping!)

HEAD STUDY

The head is the most important—and most difficult—part of drawing a horse. Give this horse a long muzzle and two alert ears. Then add an eye, nostril, mouth, and mane.

STEP 1

STEP 2

STEP 3

STEP 4

Once you've mastered the head, try drawing the rest of the horse's body.

STEP 5

CLYDESDALE

Clydesdales have bodies that are larger and thicker than those of other horses. But even though they look big and tough, these horses are actually very gentle. Draw this horse with a short tail. Cover the lower legs with long white hair called feathers.

STEP 1

STEP 2

STEP 3

STEP 4

After drawing one Clydesdale, draw a team of them pulling a sleigh through deep snow.

STEP 5

FOAL

Foals can walk right after birth and are able to gallop within a few hours. Their legs are almost as long as an adult horse's, but their hooves are much smaller. It almost looks like they're walking on tiptoe.

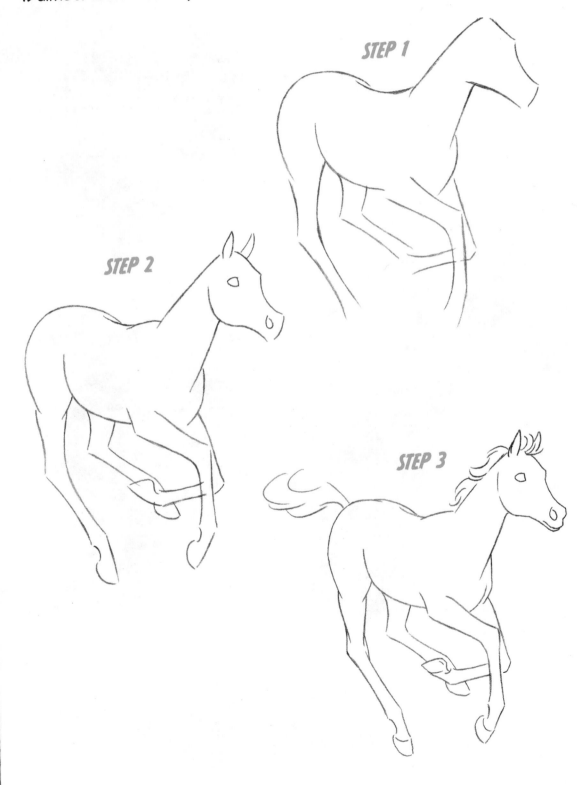

STEP 1

STEP 2

STEP 3

STEP 4

STEP 5

After drawing this frisky foal, try drawing its mother by its side.

APPALOOSA

Appaloosas are known for their spotted coats and their calm personalities. Their relaxed behavior makes them perfect horses for beginning riders. To get this Appaloosa ready for a rider, add a saddle blanket, saddle, and brindle.

STEP 1

STEP 2

STEP 3

STEP 4

STEP 5

Once you've drawn the saddle, draw yourself sitting in it, ready for a ride.

BUCKING BRONCO

You wouldn't want to take this wild bronco for a casual ride. Instead, this horse is ready to entertain large crowds at a rodeo. Draw this energetic animal with two hind legs kicking up dirt.

STEP 1

STEP 2

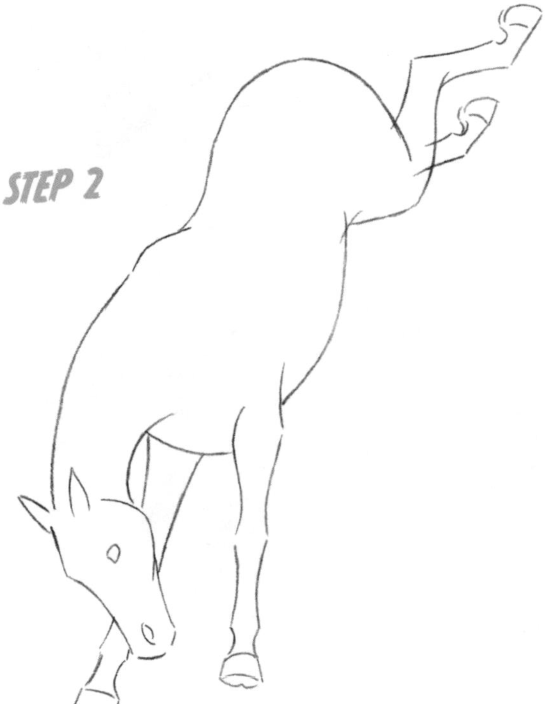

STEP 3

STEP 4

After drawing this horse, draw a rodeo cowboy taking a wild ride on it.

STEP 5

Lipizzans are shorter than most horses, but they're very strong. Their muscular legs help them perform incredible jumps and stunts to amaze audiences. Draw this horse balancing on its hind legs to perform a spinning dance.

STEP 1

STEP 2

STEP 3

EP 4

Once you've mastered this project, draw the horse leaping through the air.

STEP 5

RACING ARABIAN

Arabians are a popular breed because of their speed and endurance. Their deep chests and large nostrils allow them to run for miles. Check out this horse's mane and tail blowing wildly in the wind as she runs through falling leaves.

STEP 1

STEP 2

STEP 3

STEP 4

STEP 5

Trying drawing a herd of Arabians racing across a desert.

BRAIDED BEAUTY

Horse manes and tails were first braided to prevent them from getting pulled out while the horses worked. Now it's all about showing off at a horse show and impressing the judges.

STEP 1

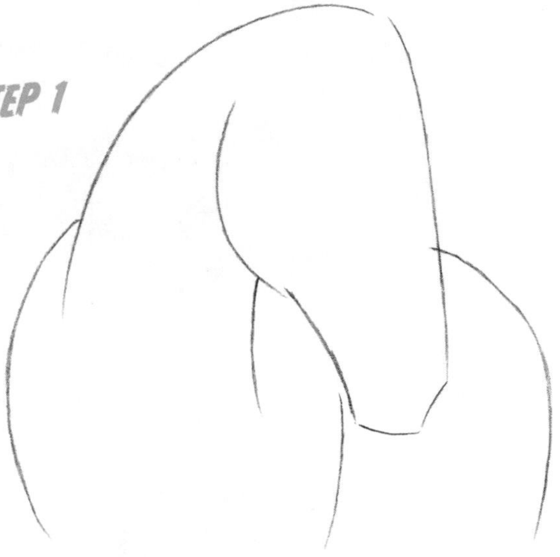

STEP 2

STEP 3

STEP 4

Once you've mastered the braids, add some colorful flowers to create a show-stopping style.

STEP 5

Thoroughbreds make great racehorses because of their speed. In fact, they're the fastest of all horse breeds. This horse and rider are competing in a show jumping competition. In this type of event, a rider takes the horse through tall jumps.

STEP 1

STEP 2

STEP 3

STEP 4

STEP 5

CONTINUED...

STEP 6

Draw the horse and rider celebrating their win. Give the rider a trophy to hold. Add a wreath of flowers around the horse's neck.

STEP 7

STEP 8

STEP 9

FACES AND BODIES

WHEN SOMEONE TELLS YOU TO DRAW A PERSON, DO YOU DRAW A STICK FIGURE? Fear not! Help has arrived! The 19 projects in this section focus on faces, fashion, and body basics. Learn how a person's facial features work together—their size, shape, and location. Take a trip through time and around the world to sketch trendy clothes. And get a feel for how the human body is proportioned and how it moves.

Keep practicing, and you'll never draw another stick figure again! Promise!

FACE FIRST

Here are the face basics that will help you with the projects in this section. Notice how this girl's eyes are halfway between the top of the head and the chin. So are her ears. Her nose fills the space between the eyes. After drawing the basics, add all the extras that make each face unique. For this girl, that means drawing lots of curly hair.

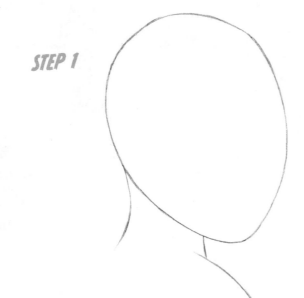

STEP 1

STEP 2

STEP 3

STEP 4

STEP 5

Now look in a mirror. Look at how each of your features fits with the others. Try drawing a self portrait.

Get ready to give this rapper's best side the star treatment. A profile shows only one side of the face, so it's a great choice if you're a beginning artist. You draw one just eye, and the nose and mouth are simple outlines. When the face is done, add a hand and a microphone to the drawing.

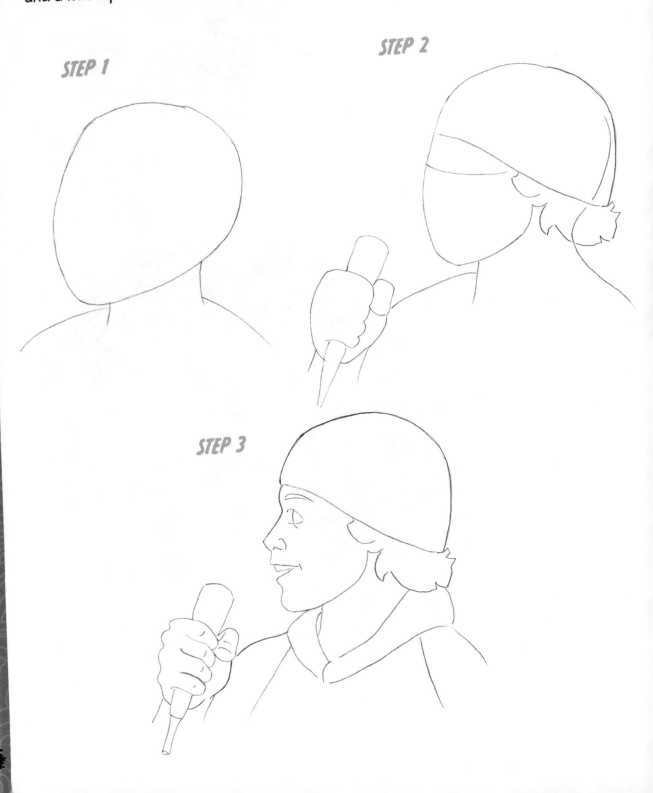

STEP 1

STEP 2

STEP 3

STEP 4

Make sure your rapper has the support he needs. Draw his backup band.

STEP 5

MANGA GIRL

Manga is a type of comic drawing that started in Japan. Its characters have distinct facial features. Large eyes and pointed chins are common. So are small noses, simple mouths, and spiky hair. This manga girl has all of these features—and a fierce attitude to match.

STEP 1

STEP 2

STEP 3

STEP 4

Play with different hairstyles for this girl. Try a long ponytail or short pigtails popping straight out of her head.

STEP 5

PICASSO ABSTRACT

Famous artist Pablo Picasso (1881-1973) drew faces with wild colors and shapes. He used an abstract style to create paintings now worth millions of dollars. Try creating your own abstract portrait. Draw a face with mismatched features and bright colors. Your drawing doesn't have to look realistic, but you should be able to tell that it's a face.

STEP 1

STEP 2

STEP 3

STEP 4

Abstract style can be used to draw almost anything. Try drawing an abstract tree, car, or cat.

STEP 5

CHIC

This clean, chic look works for everything from a shopping trip with friends to a star-studded movie premiere. It combines a crisp pair of skinny jeans and a cute cami. Complete the look with a cropped jacket in a fun, trendy color.

STEP 1

STEP 2

STEP 3

STEP 4

STEP 5

Dress up this style by switching out the jeans with a miniskirt and ankle boots.

FORMAL

Hit a glam slam with a showstopping, shimmering formal. This gown is a classic A-line shape that flares out at the waist. It's guaranteed to turn heads at weddings, proms, and all red-carpet events.

STEP 1

STEP 2

STEP 3

STEP 4

STEP 5

Formal doesn't always mean full-length. Try drawing a short A-line dress with a halter top.

1920s Retro

After all of this time, the 1920s flapper dress is still turning heads. The tiered minidress shown here is a modern version of a vintage fashion. The bright colors and knee-high boots give the look a fresh twist.

STEP 1

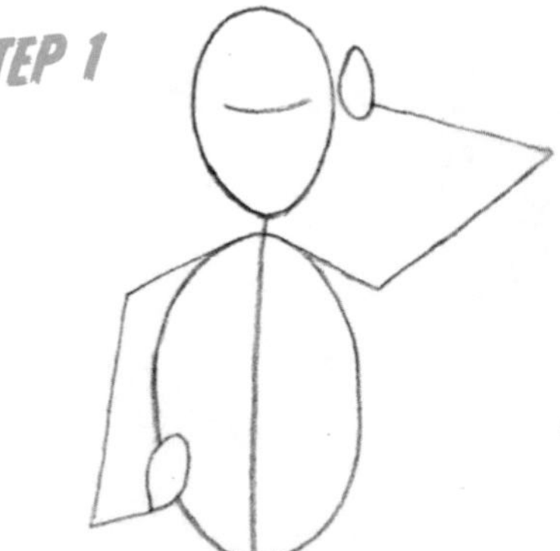

STEP 2

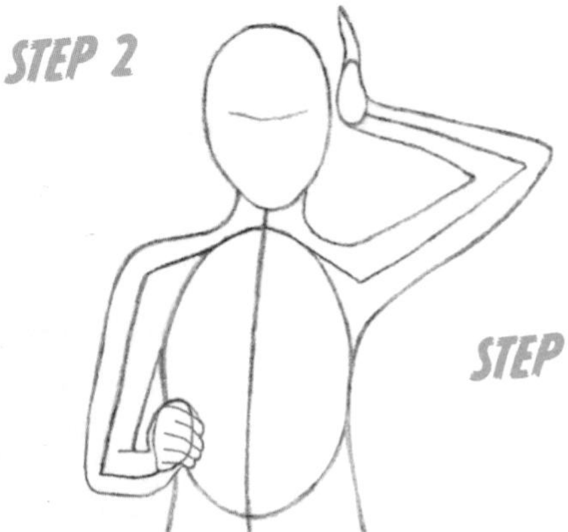

STEP 3

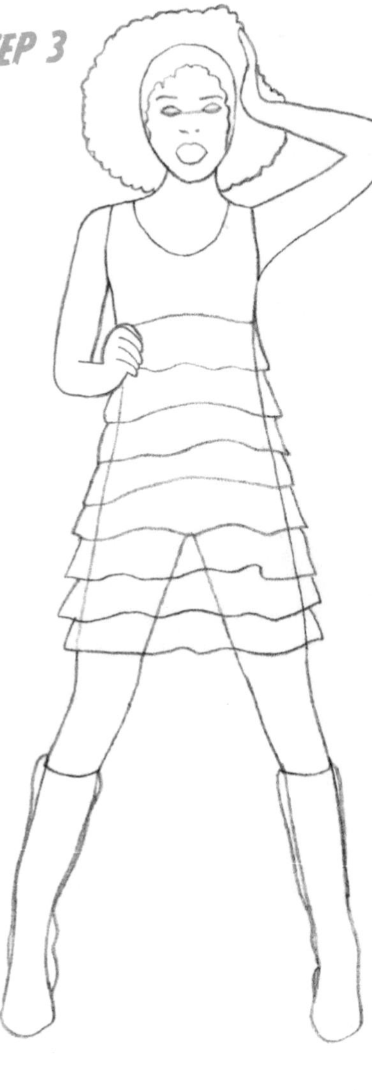

STEP 4

STEP 5

Top off this look with
a baseball cap (see
page 127) or other
type of hat.

1970s Retro

Designers love to recreate old looks and turn them into modern trends. This look borrows from the 1970s. The fringed suede boots, low-slung belt, and skinny headband are definite blasts from the past.

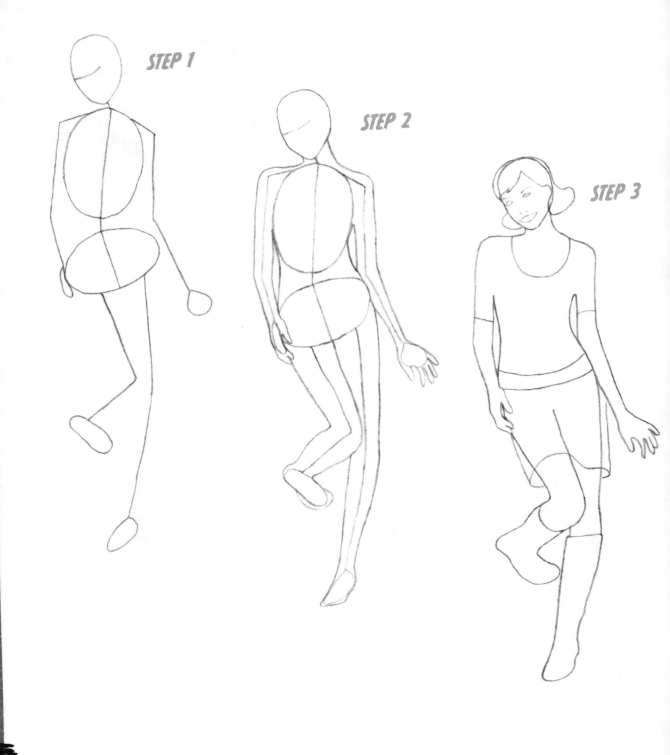

STEP 1

STEP 2

STEP 3

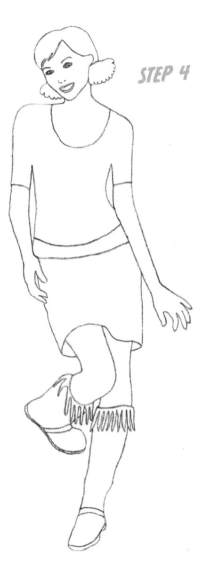

STEP 4

STEP 5

Try drawing other retro fashions, such as bell-bottom pants and platform shoes.

SUMMER

Summer is the perfect time to show off a short, sassy style. This strappy sundress does the trick. To personalize the look, add some colorful bracelets and a pair of kitten heels.

STEP 1 **STEP 2** **STEP 3**

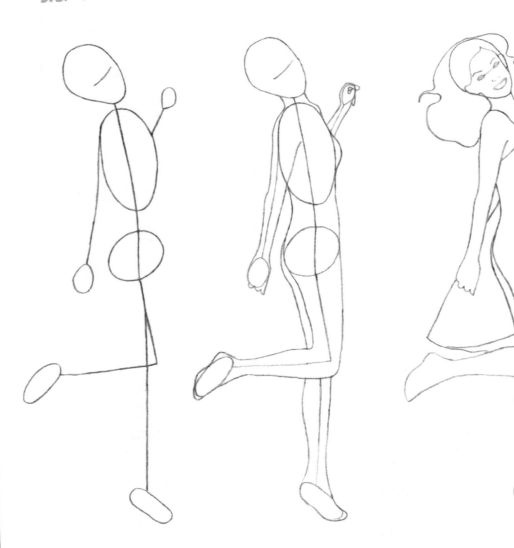

STEP 4

STEP 5

Take this look from day to night. Simply add a cropped cardigan or shrug and a patterned scarf.

WINTER

Fashion designers are all about looking cool while staying warm. The secret is lots of stylish layers. This girl is showing off a black peacoat over purple leggings. Her matching hat and gloves are practical and chic. The look is completed with a pair of boots.

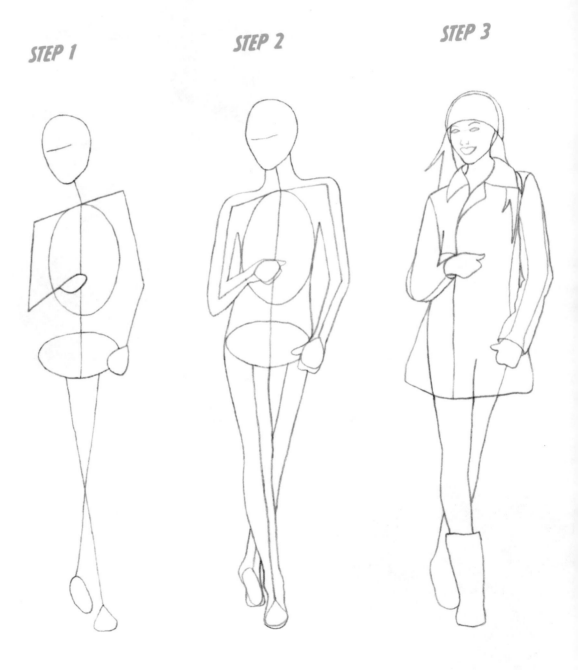

STEP 1　　　STEP 2　　　STEP 3

Try drawing a comfy sweater dress and black leggings. Don't forget the ankle boots!

GLOBAL

Every culture has something special to add to the world of fashion. This sleeveless dress takes its cue from a traditional Japanese kimono. Its bright red color and butterfly print make this global-inspired work of art hard to miss. A matching wrap completes the look.

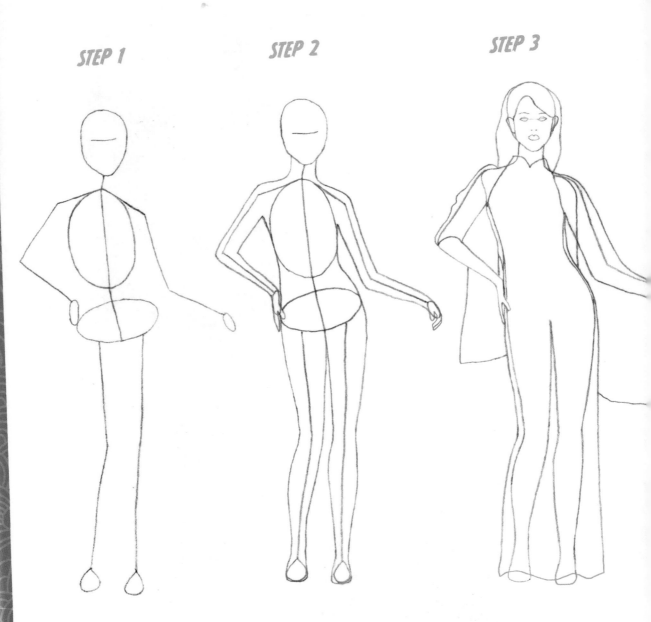

STEP 1

STEP 2

STEP 3

STEP 4

STEP 5

Add your own special design to the dress. How about birds, flowers, or snakes? Stars or swirls?

ACCESSORIES

Sometimes a cute outfit is more about the accessories than the clothes. This look starts out with a basic pair of low-rise jeans and a long-sleeved tee. Fun accessories like a colorful scarf and belt really make a statement. Add a matching purse and baseball cap for the perfect final touch.

STEP 1

STEP 2

STEP 3

STEP 4

STEP 5

Try switching out the scarf and purse with hoop earrings and a chunky necklace.

PUNK

Punk fashion comes in all kinds of variations, from hardcore to not-so-hardcore. Coordinating punk outfits make this couple a fashionable pair. He's sporting corduroy pants, a plain black tee, and a jean jacket. She's showing off a plaid skirt, athletic socks, and a combo tank top T-shirt. Both finish off their look with matching shades.

STEP 1

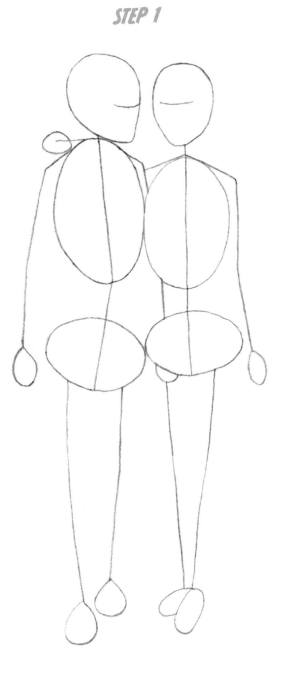

STEP 2

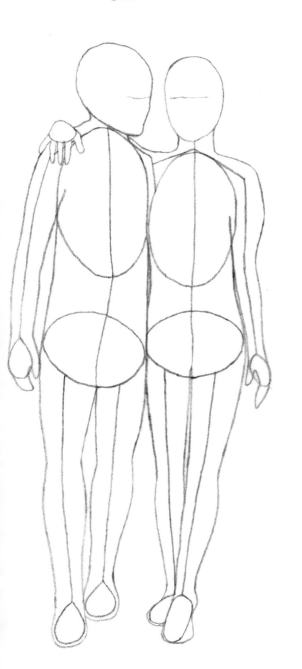

STEP 3

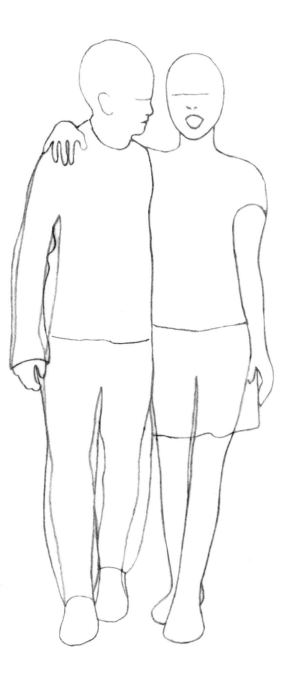

CONTINUED...

STEP 4

STEP 5

Give this couple a new look—from their hair to their feet—by creating a style that's all your own.

BALLERINA

Don't be fooled by the tights and the tutu. Ballerinas are experienced athletes. It takes strength and stamina to perform elegant arabesques and flawless pirouettes. This prima ballerina poses in a simple but graceful position.

STEP 1

STEP 2

STEP 3

STEP 4

Every great ballerina needs a place to perform. Draw a grand stage where she can show off her skills.

STEP 5

SOCCER STAR

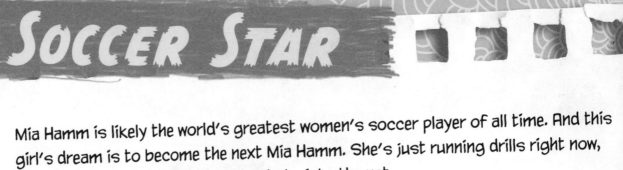

Mia Hamm is likely the world's greatest women's soccer player of all time. And this girl's dream is to become the next Mia Hamm. She's just running drills right now, but one day soon she'll be sailing shots into the net.

STEP 1

STEP 2

STEP 3

STEP 4

Draw a net and a goaltender so this player has a place to kick the ball.

STEP 5

CHEERLEADER

Get ready to pump up the crowd. Cheerleaders are all about energy, excitement, and entertainment. Make sure this well-trained athlete has a big smile and two pom-poms to wave. She'll need them later to celebrate her squad's state championship.

STEP 1

STEP 2

STEP 3

STEP 4

STEP 5

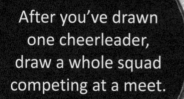

After you've drawn
one cheerleader,
draw a whole squad
competing at a meet.

PROM QUEEN

For this dancing diva, it's all about the dress. A full-length formal is the best choice for prom. That way the dress twirls around her as she dances the night away. Add a sparkling tiara to top off her look.

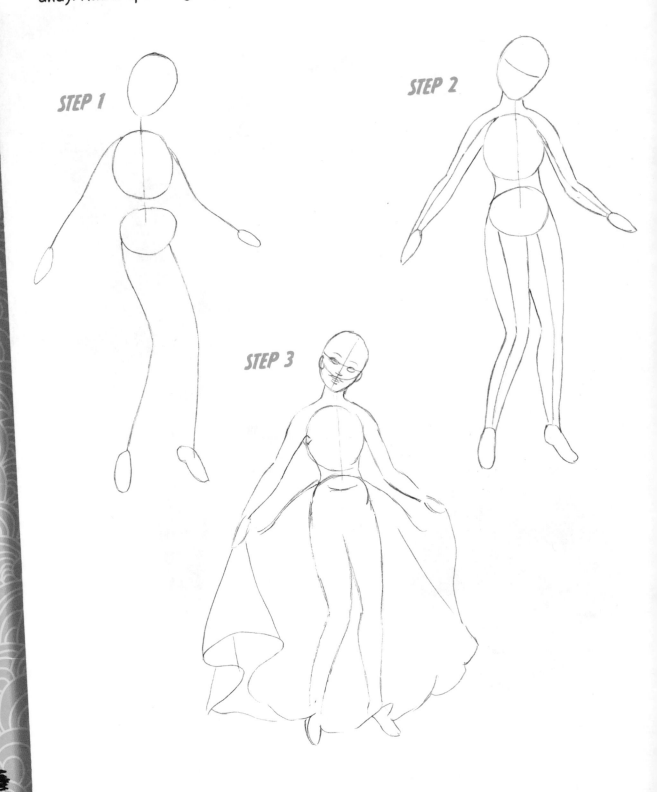

STEP 1

STEP 2

STEP 3

STEP 4

This dancing queen doesn't want to dance alone. Draw a prom king to share the spotlight.

STEP 5

SKATEBOARDER

You'll find this adventure-seeker testing her skills at the skatepark. She loves showing off kickflips and frontside boardslides. After years of practice, she thinks of her board as just another part of her, like her arms or legs.

STEP 1

STEP 2

STEP 3

STEP 4

STEP 5

Try drawing this
skater on her board,
in mid-air, coming
off a steep ramp.

MOVIE STAR

Movie stars are known for their fabulous fashion sense. This leading lady is no different. She shows off her style in a sparkling designer dress. With an elegant updo and a little bit of bling, she's ready for a red-carpet event.

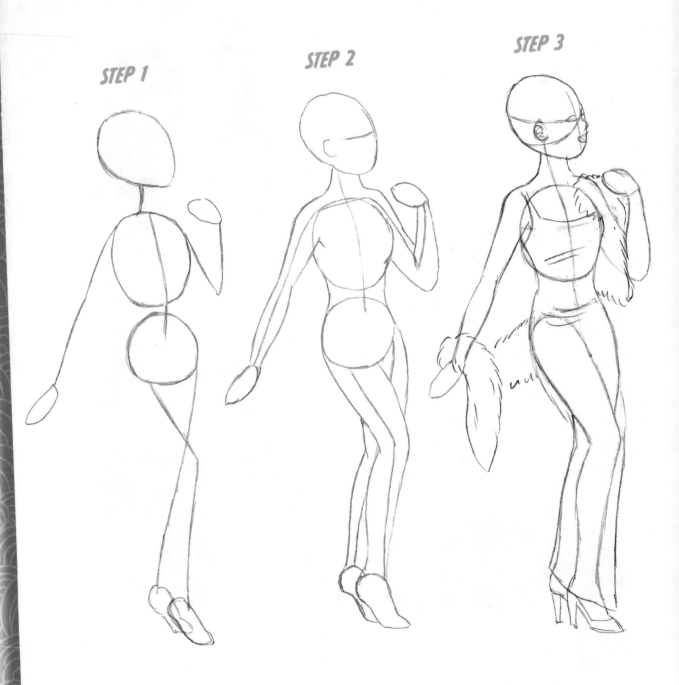

STEP 1

STEP 2

STEP 3

STEP 4

STEP 5

This diva never wears the same dress twice. Give her a new look by drawing her in a stylish short dress.

OTHER COOL STUFF

WHAT'S COOL TO YOU? Magical unicorns? Pixies dancing in a flower garden? A panda munching on bamboo or a cat napping on a shoe? How about letters of the alphabet that look like birthday cakes or candy canes?

This section is full of treats to draw, including mythical creatures, pets, and wild animals. You'll also find specially designed alphabets for scrapbooks, cards, or posters. When you're done with all 15 projects, grab some fresh paper, DIG INTO YOUR IMAGINATION, and show the world what cool means to you!

UNICORN

With a touch of their glowing horn, unicorns can heal anyone who is hurting. That's what the myths say, anyway. Maybe that's why people around the world and throughout history have spent so much time chasing after them.

STEP 1

STEP 2

STEP 3

STEP 4

Once you've drawn
your unicorn,
surround it with
a beautiful rainbow.

STEP 5

FAIRY

According to legend, fairies love to visit humans. Sometimes they fly in as twinkling spots of light in a dark room. Other times you might feel a soft breeze against your cheek as you drift off to sleep.

STEP 1

STEP 2

STEP 3

STEP 4

Draw yourself asleep in your bed, with this fairy by your head, casting a spell for sweet dreams.

STEP 5

GENIE

This genie was stuck in a bottle for a very long time. Now he's free and looking for work. If you're lucky, he might grant you a wish—maybe three! What will you wish for? Your wish is his command!

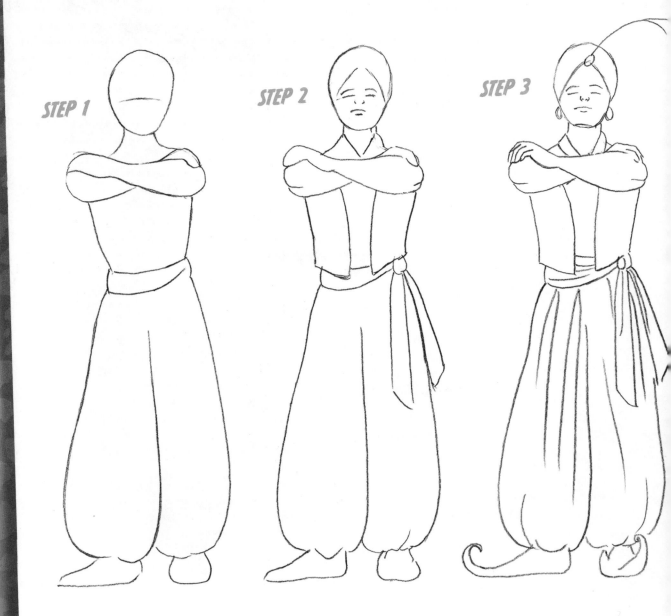

STEP 1

STEP 2

STEP 3

STEP 4

STEP 5

Draw the tall, skinny glass bottle this genie lived in. Then try drawing a magic gold lamp.

GARDEN PIXIE

Garden pixies rarely leave their flower-filled homes. They spend their days asleep on the soft petals of pansies. At night, they dance like bees, flitting from rosebud to rosebud.

STEP 1

STEP 2

STEP 3

STEP 4

Give your pixie her own garden! Visit the Flowers section, starting on page 32, to learn how to draw tulips, roses, and more.

STEP 5

DRAGON

Someone dared to disturb this fierce dragon from its sleep. Now it's awake and angry. Watch out! If it decides to use its fiery breath, you could be toast!

STEP 1

STEP 2

STEP 3

STEP 4

STEP 5

Dragons are always looking for a castle to attack. Give one to this dragon by using the drawing steps on pages 56–57.

KOALA

Get close enough to a koala and you might smell something odd—eucalyptus! Koalas live in eucalyptus trees and eat more than 1,000 leaves each day. The koalas' thick, wooly fur absorbs the leaves' strong scent.

STEP 1

STEP 2

STEP 3

STEP 4

STEP 5

Koalas sleep in trees, either hugging a branch or tucked in a tree fork. Try drawing a napping koala.

DOG

Few things are sweeter than a dog bouncing around on big, clumsy paws, eager to play. Want to go for a walk? Sure! Fetch a ball? OK! Jump in the air and catch a flying disc? You bet! This happy little guy looks ready to be your next best friend.

STEP 1

STEP 2

STEP 3

STEP 4

Love wrinkly bulldogs or tall, lean greyhounds? How about poodles? Try drawing your favorite dog breed.

STEP 5

MEERKAT

This member of the mongoose family stands straight up when it senses danger. Meerkats live in groups called mobs in the wild grasslands and deserts of southern Africa. They're always on the lookout for fierce, hungry animals roaming the savanna.

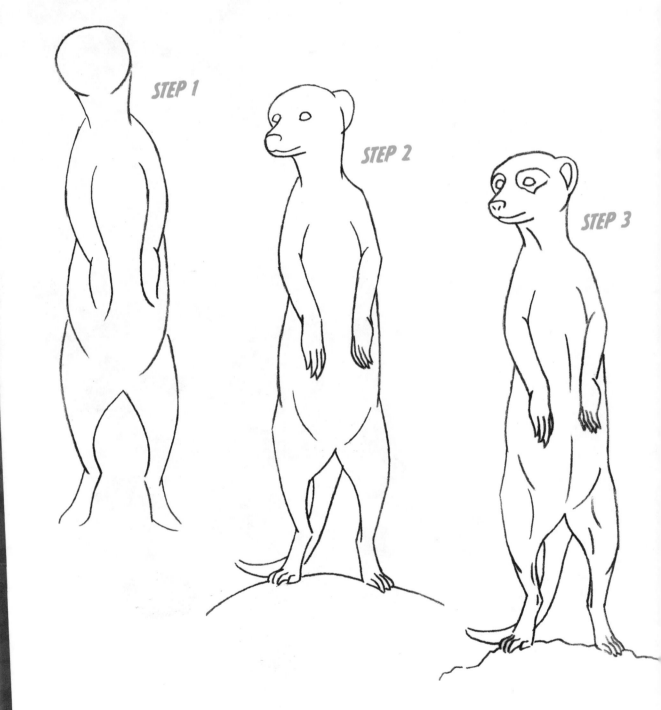

STEP 1

STEP 2

STEP 3

STEP 4

STEP 5

After you've drawn
one meerkat, draw
a mob. But grab a
big sheet of paper—
meerkats can live in
groups of 15
or more!

Cat

Cats are fun to draw because they always end up in interesting places. Sometimes they're sitting on a windowsill. Other times they're sneaking into a sock drawer. This cat chose someone's shoe as the perfect place for a little nap.

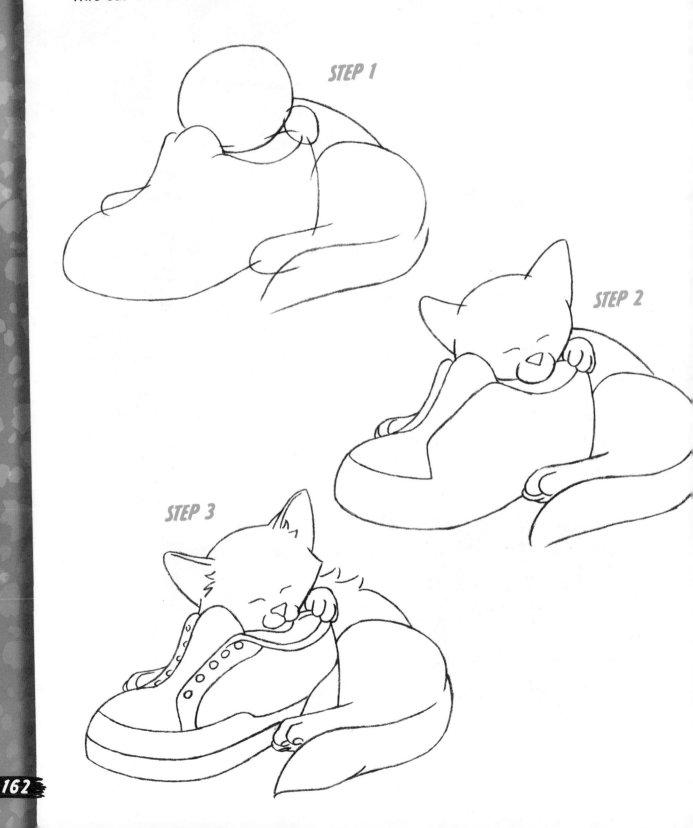

STEP 1

STEP 2

STEP 3

STEP 4

When cats aren't sleeping, they're usually playing. Draw this cat chasing a toy mouse.

STEP 5

PANDA

Pandas look like big black-and-white teddy bears. These gentle giants roam through China's bamboo forests in search of food. Each day, pandas spend more than 12 hours eating and finding food.

STEP 1

STEP 2

STEP 3

STEP 4

Once you've drawn this adult panda, draw a cub by its side. Use the steps on pages 14–15.

STEP 5

RED-EYED TREE FROG

Cute can come in all kinds of packages. Just ask the red-eyed tree frog. Sure, it's not fuzzy or cuddly. But this pint-sized amphibian wins you over with its neon green body and bright red peepers.

STEP 1

STEP 2

STEP 3

STEP 4

STEP 5

Tree frogs snag food with their long, sticky tongues. Draw your frog grabbing a moth in mid-air.

DAISY CRAZY

It's been raining all day, and you've been stuck inside. Bring the outside in with Daisy Crazy letters. Spend the day capturing your special memories in a colorful scrapbook. Grab some favorite photos and add fun, flowery captions.

STEP 1

STEP 2

STEP 3

After you've mastered daisies, try drawing each letter with a rose or a tulip. Visit the Flowers section for help.

EAT YOUR WORDS

Celebrate in style with words that look good enough to eat. Use this appetizing alphabet to create your next birthday party invitations. It's a fun way to get your guests all the important info for the big event.

STEP 1

STEP 2

STEP 3

Use your favorite food to make a new set of letters. Add chocolate sauce and cherries to create a hot-fudge sundae alphabet!

Candy canes make delicious holiday treats. But did you know they also make fun letters? Use this style to create a special gift tag for your holiday presents. Or make a big "Season's Greetings" sign for your family's front door.

STEP 1

STEP 2

STEP 3

Draw letters using other holiday items. Start with lights or snowflakes. Then create your own holiday designs.

A B C D E F G H
I J K L M N O P Q R
S T U V W X Y Z

FOR MOM

You don't have to be a cheerleader to show your school spirit. Just grab some poster board and a few markers. Add your message using the Athletic Alphabet. Then fill in the letters with your school colors.

STEP 1

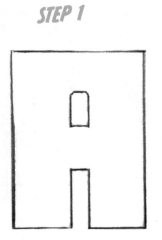

STEP 2

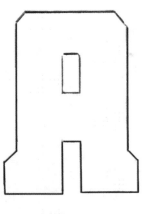

STEP 3

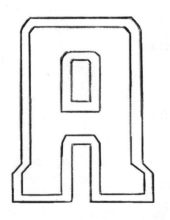

What's your favorite sport? Try coloring in the letters to look like basketballs, baseballs, or soccer balls.

A B C D E F G H I J K L M N O P Q R S T U V W X Y Z

Published by Capstone Press, 1710 Roe Crest Drive,
North Mankato, Minnesota 56003

www.mycapstone.com

Library of Congress Cataloging-in-Publication data
is available on the Library of Congress website.

ISBN: 978-1-5435-1561-9

Summary: Basic, step-by-step instructions teach
beginning artists how to draw more than 70
projects of particular interest to girls, including
animals, flowers, fairy tales, fashion, and more.

Designers: Aruna Rangarajan, Juliette Peters,
Lori Bye, Ashlee Suker, and Sarah Bennett

Image Credits: Shutterstock: all backgrounds, Jamen
Percy, 5 (color pencils and scribbles), Lifestyle
Graphic (sheet of paper), 6 and throughout, Mega
Pixel, 5 (erasers and pencil sharpener), Ruslan
Ivantsov, 5 (graphite pencil), Sanit Fuangnakhon,
cover (pencil), timquo, 5 (felt marker)

Printed in the United States   4889

WANT TO GET SERIOUS ABOUT YOUR NOTEBOOK DOODLES AND HAVE SOME REAL FUN?

If you've got love for *HORSES, BABY ANIMALS, FAIRY-TALE CREATURES, FASHION, AND MORE,* grab this book right. *The Girls' Guide to Drawing* will have you bringing more than 70 cute, cuddly, fierce, and fabulous images to life, step-by-step, in no time.

$12.95 US / $16.95 CAN

ISBN 978-1-5435-1561-9

9 781543 515619

51295

capston
www.mycapstone.c